THE MÖBIUS
STRIP CLUB
OF GRIEF

BIANCA STONE

"Bianca Stone is a brilliant transcriber of her
generation's emerging pathology and sensibility."

—JOHN ASHBERY

"Bianca Stone's *What is Otherwise Infinite* is a majestic exploration in what it means to be alive. Interspersed between tender and grotesque descriptions of everyday and domestic life, the reader finds something holy here. There are the immortal voices of those thinkers and poets from the past who inform the landscape of the book, both mentally and spiritually. There are the haunting traces of the eternal present and of the possible future that seethe their resentment, regret, and even joy everywhere. There is also a human heart within the book beating so relentlessly that you can tell the time by it. But more than any of this, there is language here— real poetry—that transforms your way of seeing the world with its terrifyingly beautiful presence. This is a legendary book. It will change you. You must read it."

—DOROTHEA LASKY

"Bianca Stone is a seeker. Wry, funny, and often thwarted, mired in daily life, metaphysically tormented, afflicted by what she calls 'allergies of the soul,' she searches for something deep and meaningful, something ongoing, mysterious, and ineffable. She has the impulse to kneel and be 'thunderstruck with language,' to find 'the new Eucharist,' to call out to a God who is also searching for God. *What is Otherwise Infinite* is a rare thing in contemporary American poetry— a spiritual testament."

—EDWARD HIRSCH

WHAT IS OTHERWISE INFINITE

Published by Tin House, Portland, Oregon

Distributed by W. W. Norton & Company

Library of Congress Cataloging-in-Publication Data

Names: Stone, Bianca, author.
Title: What is otherwise infinite : poems / Bianca Stone.
Description: Portland, Oregon : Tin House, [2022]
Identifiers: LCCN 2021042864 | ISBN 9781951142971 (paperback) |
   ISBN 9781953534057 (ebook)
Subjects: LCGFT: Poetry.
Classification: LCC PS3619.T65643 W48 2022 | DDC 811/.6—dc23
LC record available at https://lccn.loc.gov/2021042864

First US Edition 2022
Printed in the USA
Interior design by Jakob Vala

www.tinhouse.com

"The Cry" from *The Selected Levis* by Larry Levis, selected by David St. John, © 2000. Reprinted by permission of the University of Pittsburgh Press.

WHAT IS OTHERWISE INFINITE

BIANCA STONE

TIN HOUSE / Portland, Oregon

for
Odette, Walter, and Ben

Contents

TRIAD

TETRAD

WHAT IS OTHERWISE INFINITE

Human Nature

Why is it, our
                exhibition (forgive us our) pleasure, gazing
into enormous paintings of lost battles,
the naked raped townspeople piled on the dying horses
and the indifferent pastures and frescoes of gods, gossamer gray
yet unhaunted snow; forgive us the glossaries, lists,
barely discernible woodcuts of the tortured—

I have proclivities, forgive me,
for bittersweet liquids stirred with the poisoned hatpin;
staggering brass, finials and knobs, all patina,
Valium caught in the satin lining of a mother's purse—
a dead ladybug like a charm on the windowsill
and its underwings spread open for the Annunciation—

forgive me how I carry the spaces
between self-hatred and magnificence
between my breasts
through the metal detector I will never clear—that
a typical day is fatalism and utopia. That
I deal only in the hardest pain-revivers, symbols,
and tongues. That it makes no sense unless you look at it
sideways, like a hen—that I want to tell you only
in the intimacy of our discomfort.
That it is because

I haven't been touched nearly enough in one lifetime
to be satisfied—and now want you,
across all this dead gauze,
to put your lips

        to mine.

MONAD

The mind is its own place, and in itself
Can make a Heaven of Hell, a Hell of Heaven.
What matter where, if I be still the same,
And what I should be, all but less than He
Whom thunder hath made greater?

—John Milton, *Paradise Lost*

Marcus Aurelius

Sometimes I wake in the night
in a headache, my mouth like an iron forge,
looking for anything valuable in the debris.
I turn on the tiny light clipped to my book,
I write things down
in the spirit of Marcus Aurelius
who said the finest bottle of wine
is nothing but grape juice passing through the liver.
No matter the beauty of a frosted glass
or a night of big Truth-seeking, never recalled,
the importance of putting something sweet
into our mouths, turning it around and around
on our tongues, attaching to it our missions,
our purpose—in the end
we are all just filters. No more miraculous
then the plainest of birds. Who, up close,
we can hardly believe,
nor as focused as the deer tick—
nothing is given over to, nothing new is lit.
So often it is this. I wake up, urgent, fatalistic,
with the taste of nectar on my boughs.
I replay on a loop my one stoic consistency,
my middle-of-the-night vow
that I will start tomorrow
the essential dismantling
of how I live.

Routine

Some days I get up to go for a run
but instead just sit in spandex
and write about the fog.
Is the fog lifting or the trees rising?
Who cares. Nature transfers her blood
into the air. We are her lung cancer.
Her trans fat. Her addiction.

Some days I get up early to write
but instead clean—the great lie
that I am doing something.
The horrible way ketchup keeps, still bright;
beer cans lined up on the porch railing.

It is the end of the summer.
The insects are at their biggest.
They bang and thrum against the screens,
maniacs, giving their last hurrah.
I creep around like Nancy Drew
with my hunch and no real proof.
All things feel preordained, repeated.
My body is numb. Without anticipation.
I sit in the lobby of someone else's potential
thinking it is my own. I go about my day
convinced I am immortal.

Does Life Exist Independent of Its Form?

What is immortal?
And if it is immortal how is it that
it has an incurable disease
and wanders around
a total aberration, a mutant, while
the catamount vanishes from the species.
Is it that we live at the top of the food chain, alone
with no link to anything above us,
no elegant forfeiture in the mouth of the tiger?
Or is our problem that
we do not actually live
at the top of the food chain.
And are devoured daily by thought. And time.
Holy and obscene; unmentionable.

Time does not go beyond its maiden name.
And anyway, right now, everything tastes good.
All the male poets' poems, and dirty, dirty chocolate layer cake.
I swallow it with a glass of milk.
The crumb crawls down my throat
and enters me. The power of Christ compels,
        not I—but the wish to be changed—
everything is challenged
by the sudden flame of joy—
how uncomfortable we are with happiness.

But Darling, you're staggering.
Your temple mouth is being forsworn.
Sister, crying in the hammock
because your lover will not come—
the children are screaming and running with blue guns
in the air, with little cuts on their feet.

And you, little mole angel, restless song,
smashed idol, bronzed cat head
on the hood of a car headed into the ravine
driven by our ancestor's dark awe of a comet—

how can someone *not* become
heartbreaking in one sense
of the word—not find
they are a stranger   in their own household
of truly
          unnamable need?

Nature

Maybe humans are the failed AI of Nature.
Maybe Nature made something it thought would tend the garden.
Maybe Nature made something sexy, to watch
clean the pools with long butterfly nets
and a sunburn—the retainers of Nature.
Now, mirror of mercury and Hell, that hot-red bomb
in your mouth, that sweet battleground on your tongue—
it is the catastrophe of your mission.
The wealthy, with their outstanding educations
and custom shoes and empty apartments,
floating above like Glinda; the ballad of media,
the intellectuals, almost shepherding
evolution, falling asleep in their haunted paintings
and unattainable poetry—all the dimensions
of each person's being, punk, restless in a loop.

Sometimes, I want to be taken into nothingness.
I want to be burned with the gypsy moths and bindweed.
Run to exhaustion with the wildebeest.
I don't want this phone; I want to kill God.
Maybe humans are the complex systems
of a natural order that must build and destroy itself
in perpetuity. Blue chicory on the road
in a sandstorm of our passing—they gyrate and smile—

what of our little duties to the architect?
Our deep red blood, our lush tech—
Archangels, limping in paradise.

Apocrypha

It is said that Jesus couldn't admit to himself that he was a simile.
That he hung out with tax collectors and whores.
That he was profound allegory and data compression.
He said he'd "explain later" but rarely did.
He fostered over a billion abandoned children.
Whenever he saw someone
remodeling a home
he would volunteer his skills, sanding the drywall
until the seam was virtually seamless.
They say he was jealous of Osiris.
That the last thing he sucked on
was vinegar from a sponge lifted from a hyssop plant.

And who can explain it to the Literalists?
He said no man could spiritually mature
without being also a woman,
no woman without becoming a man.
"Peter hates all of my sex," Mary Magdalene wept to him one day.
Whenever Jesus saw a horse standing in a field in the rain
totally still, with its eyes closed,
he fell into a depression
because he knew he would never lead humanity through such
    an education.
They say his favorite thing to do on Passover
was dunk the egg in saltwater

and feed it to Mary.
They say that a man named Simon
also went around calling himself Christ, suffered in Judaea,
and paired with a "redeemed harlot."
It was common knowledge that Jesus was everyone.
Loved Mary Magdalene best out of all the disciples.
That all the women surrounding him were named Mary.
Confusing on purpose. That the myth
was created to make a tangible basis for comparison.
That because of him
Rilke thought life was a series of coded
messages, and in conversation Rilke spoke
as if in spells, as naturally as adverbs.

And anyway, we are all various manifestations of THAT.
Like a fungus. We are the fruit
of a mycorrhizal network
linking plants through minute cords of mycelium.

They say that God
is the oldest tree in the universe.
That Jesus was simply a Douglas fir.
That in the beginning a stone was flung into the air
and it snapped into a bird that made the song
of a phone ringing. That the bird shat

on the head of a primeval woman
who was giving birth to fraternal twins in a field of thistles.
That each twin went out into the world
dazed, ignorant, lost. That that was all
part of the great big Plan.
They say that relative to our desires
our goodness is overwhelming. That living is tragicomedy.
That we seek what is good for a limited idea of Good.
And we should go bigger.
That we were unsavable. But already saved.
That we partied so well.
That we never had—through the wall—to confess.
That we were forgiven from birth.
And it was just a matter of remembering.

God Searches for God

Of my unclear and unimaginable self
I want none of it. There is nothing
higher than I. Only monks at my feet kissing warts.
I have nothing to give but tears, of which one
is too much and a whole sea
not enough. Do not fathom me here.
Do not touch this. Having laid the cosmic egg
who will take my eternal life in their hands?
It is said this planet came to be
when I was pulled apart.

The Human Good

Human nature tries to weave the naked cloth of saints
so thin it barely feels it. Our nature is tired of looking
for meaning. It wants to go indoors. Watch some television.
Sleep on the couch covered in little sharp crumbs.

Our nature tries to establish the right boundaries.
Tries to make some S.M.A.R.T. goals.
Only gets fatter. Poorer. Nothing
can be relied upon but the disappointment
of beer. The parables of wealth.
And human nature can't even stop
to examine progress. Because by now
it is trying something new. (Human nature
is always moving on to the next big thing.)

Meanwhile, life thunders along.
With no clear purpose. No end in sight.
We settle in to read aloud the linguistic eloquence of obscure
contemporary fucking poetry. The pitfalls of Descartes's
dualism. The anarchy of flesh. The anxiety of goodness.
This will give us some idea of what's to come,
we say confidently, gathering around ourselves
the magazines of cutting-edge
sorrow, of effort, of words.
Surely this is *it*.

The Legend of the One-Headed Woman

It's totally normal
the way you can waste your life
trying to fix your life.

I don't care to translate what it means.
Laid bare by the vulturine wind,
a sparrow caught in its terrible mood.

I know something essential is there.
I do not know what to do.
My lust for something other than this—

filling the vents and veins to the shocked mainframe
with candy and lamplight
until the whole system slows to a crawl

towards the bed
where it fades into a pattern
almost indiscernible from the duvet cover

of our poorly rendered stars.

The Malady

It's allergies of the soul. When it's too late you notice
your face has fallen. Pills moved around in your hand.
You don't know where you are. Or what you've done
with your time, which you know is unfathomably precious,
but you're not sure in what way, or what to do with it.

And I suspect when you read this it will have already taken me.
Even now, it knows I know. It watches through the very young
who have so recently escaped the overwhelming original cure
and come into this world. My toddler climbs up on a rock
and turns to look at me. She sees how I suffer from it.
How I slink from screen to screen with it.
How my books will not come to fruition because of it.
How it keeps me from ever being enough.

Drunk during Creation

You rise naked from all things chaos
to tear the sea from the sky;
you rub your hands together
to make fire—mountains, rivers,
metal, the reefs and crows
wandering for a name.
Your sloppy hands forge
luxurious breasts, balls,
tight in a Babylonian fervor,
no memory whatsoever
of the invention
of what now
is only the platypus:
pelt and quilt with a duck bill
born with ankle spurs
of venom and an electric eyeball—you were
a sadist even then, knowing
the structure of pleasure and pain.
In those inspired moments
you hardly knew
what to call yourself.
In those blackouts
joy sat upon your face
like a loose mask

and you feasted on the last
of the unicorns
and licked the wings off Man.

I'll Tell You

No human
should be this desolate
and tired all the time.
Moving with the flies
around Pigpen, minor
grubby character
from *Peanuts*,
my golem,
mistaking the swarm
for a great time.
It is a jewel of end
by the end of every day—
oh dear,
I keep thinking I get it
and I will tell you about it
but there is nothing to tell
apparently
nothing concrete anyway;
they say that is the way
with the great ineffable mystery:
to believe in nothing
makes no difference

my sister tells me things
that frighten me
what I mean is
how did we get here
made of gingerbread in the oven
eaten by the mother
eaten by the wolf
my little pale nephew standing on the porch
explaining lava in the netherworld
that if you fall in a certain hole
in his game
you keep falling forever
and you don't get to keep
any of the things
you made.

Alcohol

I am a poor alcoholic standing by the door
asking everyone not to drive
or if they read Lorca's metaphysical cry as torment or

resounding ecstasy, embroidering his name
on his mother's white death pillow, like Proust
in this respect, Mother always at the ready, always dying in
    him, her kisses torn

between the teeth like a piece of fresh bread.
My eyes hurt to think about it. I'm drinking in the abandoned
burning vineyard of a fur coat in the dark, watching
the firewall coming toward me—I think I see my father there,

fervent, slobbering,
I am speaking of course of pain,
for I am also the poor parishioner standing by the door
asking if Millay ever found a mouthful of peace

and everyone is starting to sing, my hands
on the guitar, my head behind a curtain,
my boots in the deep recesses of the past—I'll admit,

I'm never the last standing; mostly, I ghost,
exiting without a word, upstairs into my little field
to wait out the crowd, listening to them,
almost making out their words, reemerging later

with a mop and a bucket when everyone is gone,
I always feel I must at least turn off all the lights;
I don't know if it is necessary

to crucify oneself every single day
or only when reaching the very bottom—

Oh but I know *you*.
One establishes an autocracy with you. You age. As old
as slime itself. As old as the first puddle. And you look it,
suddenly, when I stare into a bathroom mirror
grounding back into the usual unbearableness of the body—

something supreme, cut away from the whole—

we only ever wanted to bring you back down
from your dizzying inevitable ascent.
And it never works. Once you're off, you're off.
That's how it is, depending on another life-form.
Depending on ichor; to think you can hold fire—

you are the wrong bridal chamber stumbled into; strained
and striped, with your own concussed
double vision of splendor—you look
gorgeous in theory—
you widow me every time.

After Getting Advice to Look out the Window & Say "Thank You"

An apple tree in the snow.
And an apple
that never fell, clinging
to a branch at the top.
For Bashō it would be settled.
But I'm of a mind
to incite Aristotle's tragic
plot structure
that I must purge pity;
withered, frozen
inane and useless
with each puff of breath
while this tree, mistaken for biblical
with pitched fingers
dappled in warts and jewel,
sways the loam of bark
into a sky where no thing asks
to be born
but is
(immeasurably small) in
luxury—

I think
all things look
average to one another
where there is
astonishment raving
not so much
as to tremble—
I think some mistakes
are made with no greater
purpose than this.

The Way Things Were Until Now

I am bored of all the excuses.
Bored as Mayakovsky
at the Finnish painters' exhibition
barking like a dog through the foreign minister's toast
until he cried and sat down. Deadly serious.
I am bored as an elegy. I mean,
why care at all, speaking as a pitfall
in a world of pits. But we do. To the death.
We all agree to garden this year.
And my raspberry bushes,
picked over by wrens—
I'll make them great again
and let America go wild.
It'll be all trumpets and leeks and lilacs
from here on out.
Let's stop paying for it, get it free.
Let's plan our victory gardens to supplement grief,
boost morale, as though something new
and uncontrolled were available—
it is the original new hot future joy.
We're making it out of dough.
And the illusion of separateness,
let it go back into remission.
Just look at you—you look
like a resurrected child.

A serious drama in a cosmic joke.
Scarred, masked, dangerous.
And what of the new Eucharist?
How hungry I always am. How I long to lack.
Though in Walmart
my heart beats a little faster.
I want the world to heal up.
And the world is a field—as if it were indeed flat, curving
and caving, as if it were a piece of paper,
a Gustave Doré engraving
from the *Divina commedia*,
the one with the silhouettes of Dante and Beatrice
standing in front of the blinding
exploding white rose
that you realize when looking more closely
is all made up of bodies and wings twisting together;
the "saintly throng," they call it, mashed and hurtling,
an image of Heaven, and the creation of angels, though it is
frenzied as any image of Hell, around a divine nipple,
Odin's lost eye in the well, the drain to the other side,
joy that gets more frantic
the more you try to quiet it down.

Illuminations

I found the purpose of the earlier scenes,
the Saint's passion, for instance, bound to a diagonal cross
(in order to differentiate him from Christ),
meaningless, but necessary.
That Saint died after no more than three
days of torment. But there are full-page miniatures now
in his honor, in the Books of Hours, splayed in a diffident
specter-like cheer, his arms upraised, the crowd
numb and low and engrossed—
Human nature is bifolios, versos, even blank pages
with preparatory rulings for the scribes, never painted upon.
Little books of suffering saints and resurrections.
That's what we are.

Remember that errors will be made.
Even in our laboriously created books:
(the ox, traditionally associated with Luke,
shown above Matthew), (the origin of the bear
at the Annunciation, problematical). On this sheet
the Evangelist dips a pen into an inkpot
and rests an arm on the side of a chair,
inspired, like Luke, by the dove,
preparing to set down an account of a life
on paper made from the skin of sheep.

The artist will demonstrate understanding
for the interpretation of receding space,
the progressively diminishing size of this conceit;
the depiction of the centrally placed coffin in this book,
covered with a gold-patterned black pall and white cross
will mean something other. Something unutterable.

The artist will look upon the bat for no purpose.
A mammal of the order Chiroptera.
And like the angel, every bat is terrifying.
They keep appearing in my house,
silent and graceful, and so too as in Rilke's elegy,
we stand in the doorframe with coats over our heads
and fishing nets in our hands, asking, Who *are* you?
And so too, in the center of the village of
Brandon, Vermont, I will stand at a railing
and watch a bat come out from under the bridge
over the water that moves to fall, tumbling, magnificent,
endlessly into the ravine—
I will watch the bat that seems
like an ecstatic shadow of Rilke himself, circling
and circling the bearing strata, underneath the small span
of bridge, its brown-veined knife-like wing turning sideways
like a *Star Wars* ship, disturbing the surface of the water
with the sharp edge, the ripple moving out from the touch

as delicate as would an eyelash falling off the eye of a saint
        onto the water.

All nature is the guts of goats, hammered into paper
and painted with images of tortured pagans.

Perhaps the design I should consider is the stone, not the flesh.
No nutrition attached. No life. Not brought here by hunger
but the bone result
of all that desire that came before.
(The vivid colors of Books of Hours were sometimes
from semiprecious stones, gold, and egg.)

Consider the scene of the Virgin Mary
visiting her cousin Elizabeth, how
it is surrounded like our heads, by a droll,
grotesque marginalia.
A human half-figure fends off butterflies
with a sword. A snail attacks a tower. Behind them
the walled-in medieval city. The flayed sun.

When I am like this, I can taste
the earth by just looking at it,
like pregnant women who crave dirt, a gesture of animalism—I,
wanting to die, wanting to dig back in,

in a perpetual calendar of demise and resurrection,
want to put stones in my mouth.
Want to taste something of rock.
I'm stuck inside the walls of a secret garden
that hasn't been tended in many years, maybe ever.
Its roses contort, the terminal buds gone amok—
it is some version of the feral, original state
after being tampered with: gardens left alone.

Sometimes you pass a house in Vermont long abandoned
and sinking into the ground,
and there will still be, every spring, daffodils
within the mass of weeds and new forest—
where someone once cultivated and controlled nature,
developed flower beds into specific patterns—
come back like bright, natural scars.

I dream I lay grief on a tarp by the highway, for sale,
for practically free. And wait.
I dream I go to the jail to turn myself in,
but at the last moment, turn away,
and live my life.

A page turns, stiff and adorned.
The painted pains we stand before, wait upon, pray to,
all the devotion to it, as if the slaughter
is all we can hope for, the living, smashed into pigment
and spread between the eyes of the young—
inheriting over and over again
the beautiful, upside-down fading look of saints.

DYAD

Artichokes

I bet I'll never appear in a dream or a summer dress
or next door. Displaying on one hand my prowess, on the other
my difficultness, I bet there will be just enough pain
to keep me alive, long enough for the moon to be mine,
just as the sea is of women: the cockle, the star,
and the movements of the earth. Just as
the whale, stuck in its baleen grin, climbs up
out of the depths and moves to its hidden
spawning grounds—

I don't know. What is it to be seen? I can forget
it's language I long for. Man and his ciphers
cannot save me. Meaning cannot not pile me up
with more meaning. I go off like a firework
in the yard. I take the limbs off myself
and club the air—for the dead women of television
displayed artistically in the woods, for the details
of their reddish hair, for their always pale white skin,
their now foul,
ravaged cunts—do you have to be thus
to be avenged? I don't know.

I've seen the last of it: an ache.
To be saved. There are wildfires
switching course to worry about.
I take my daughter to the lake and watch her feel the tiny waves.
A seagull lifts a sandwich right from my hands.
I take out my tired breast. And of having felt
like a small event for so long—having felt
like an artichoke, scraped away at with the front teeth,
one scale at a time, worked down
to the meaty heart, but with the ultimate
disappointment of meager flesh—
of being thus, I bet I will live again.
I bet I will appear in full gear, the armor
of ugly indefinite livability, the real body,
alive or in decay—I'll appear
like a thundering, I'll save
myself. And you. And you.

Autobiography

I didn't come
from the fresh jelly of the body.
Mold grew me.
Engulfed. The flowers overgrew.
Poetic affluence acquired me on the cheap.
Chairs broke me, bags of clothes
and papers left too long in sheds,
the smell of their blight
was the smell of my youth.
Anonymous fetid colonies built the embryo
in its damp quilts and soft books.
I aged into being like a prison alcohol
in the back of a toilet, fatherless;
the first puddle never stirred.
It was a toadstool that decided my sex.
A symbiotic colony of bacteria
coaxed me out
of ignorance into ignorance.

The Body

I am tired of algorithms.
I was promised oblivion!
Now I must remake world order.
Nothing changes.
All these nerves and
yellow lacy fat.
It hides in a stupor
in plain sight.
I yank it around like a mule.
Cannot live by it . . .
What is it,
what is it
but a stained document
you turn in
to the school nurse

a parchment
you've been
clutching forever
that turns out blank?

The Way Mirrors Happen

Going up the stairs of your house with laundry
like one of the washers
of the Magdalene asylums for fallen women,
you pass the tall, always unclear mirror
and glance quickly at yourself, meeting your eyes,
like a waitress commiserating by sight
with the only other waitress
at the steakhouse of off-duty men.
A whole needlecraft passes between you,
a fleeting empathy that hardens and endures.

Your job has become a conduit of static electricity.
Wrinkled tea towel, faded underwear.
You are both undercover
in the Domestic Tragedies Department
playing housewife. That you are somehow not separate
from your reflection
cannot fully resolve in your heads.
And it is a weird comfort.
To think one of you
will no longer look out
after the other has collapsed.

Fasting

Empty as Jesus
after forty days in the desert
with what he thought was the Devil
but really was just himself
coming down off humans.

What do I know about it.
I wish I could not even leave
this room.

The largest of creatures is the mushroom
spreading its torn pimples
across a mass of acreage
the sun subsumes to a smear each day.

Between species there is a feeling.

It doesn't even matter, Albert Einstein's annoyance
at the stupidity of everyone around him
to the point of cruelty. It doesn't matter
that there is no God
but this palimpsest,
this archaic gold skull in your skull.

I can see the hoary clusters of stars.
I am not absent from bone fossils
and infinity.
Resolve is a machine of cold air.

Psychodynamic Motivational Speech

On my last night as a child, that sleep was final.

—Larry Levis, "The Cry"

I love the way the great mystery looks back at itself
in horror. The elementary school
keeps improving, as if your childhood were one big fire hazard.

You can almost see yourself, waiting there on the curb
with your little stained backpack
and that

disastrous stare you were developing,
already affixed to your brow; knowing
that no one is coming
except the primal departed
in an eternal, salubrious nuptial—

nothing is coming for you, you know now,
but the sparrow black wind,
an endless depression; fossil and pitted expanse of skin—

in the meantime
there are so many things to think about, to thank.

The shadow that does what you are loath to do.
Bird-bone whistle, whittled by the first bard,
blown for the first time
for the success of a newborn's first bowel movement—

you, stuck in the neurotic house's cerebral files,
the wardrobes,
                    in astonished shame,
and the wallpapered drawers like flower-lined coffins.

And like words, the closets will carry obligations.

Now let me tell you something: Shame is spent.
Empty. Redundant.
Let's look at this for a minute. You, who present

                    a totally deluded clown
wandering drunkenly up
and down the squalid street, scaring everyone.
You, who present the ugly, tragic
petulant child, who can't stand the thought of being wrong—

it is the only wrong thing you've done,
saying you're wrong
over and over again.

That's purgatory, baby.   Can you see that?

Can you look me in the eye and tell me? Detached
as you are from the room—can you
tell me where it appears in you? I'm here to wait.

Praying in the leafless wood—I get it: stuck looking
at the destroyer every time you look in a mirror.
The long hours of it. The halogen views of it.

The way you carry a wall in your face
like Ophelia not cast

as Ophelia
                    but as the nameless Chorus—

I get it—that you believe you must flounder
each day
let ichor
from the eye
from the arm
from the lips—

you get to watch your own suicide offscreen
every day

        you get to clean up the flowers after every take—

I mean,
        what do I know about shame,
being only the madness you leaped from?

I know it will let itself in.
It will handle, roughly, the tiny glass animals on the mantel.
Break the ears off, the tails. The delicate edges. I know

that shame
        lessens the value of things, the truth of things,
not the opposite. Now tell me how sustainable that guest is.
How long-term that is.

Is any of this landing?
Can I get an Amen from you?

And between the whole plasticky
currency of memory, opened now like a ripped menu,
tell me, what you would have—
now that you've looked back,
now that you can look back

at *me*, divine and unavailable—

when will you put
lavender in the linen,
with the selected works of Goethe, opened on your bed
like you were punishable

      for your own frozen, Faustian nature—a pocketknife
          in your hand,
the flesh, shoved against the crypt's corner
and the fingers of the dead in your mouth—tell me what good
  is *that*

misdirected wrath? Glinting and flickering and blue

like a TV in an empty room;

howling in someone else's hallway for a hundred years—
is this coming though?

How long

      is this going to take? Would you

put my whole, wounded body in your own,   if I asked you?

Where is your anger?

(I would love that animus, bridge between sexes, that
stranger with a face like a young lion—nothing can
      touch it, manifesting in whole arias, antidotes
from that joy devil.)
What of it? Just to the end of time?

What of it?

You can grow old this way.
What of it?

Oh, you can definitely *go on like this.*

Stepping out into the street in Rutland, across from the bus
    stop where a painkiller couple sits
with their wallets and cigarettes and socks in plastic bags,
smoking in the cold wind, complaining about—something,
    muffled—they
are more content, it seems, than you,

in your blue coat that falls open
and shows all the gold watches of men hidden there,

their cracked glass, their cocks toward midnight,
oxidized into place—can you, leading yourself
out—overgrown child as you are—tell the difference?

Perseus, looking in the mirror at what
could not be seen directly—and Medusa, bound in a statue;
    bound to her own stone—

you, aimed at the floor,

        can you tell the difference?

Yield

Get down on your knees and be thunderstruck with language.
Start in like those fanatics you read about

who stop eating and drinking and live
on the breath of irises, heavy mist.

I can hear the beat   against your head—

you look like a broken porcelain cup
        swept into a bag so it won't hurt anyone else.

And you look lit on fire, buried in the ground;

like a bad
             omen   you appear, burned, barren,

barely tethered

        to anything whole—

and where are you now? Out the window again.

        Sucked into your own reflection there.

It is not even your own affliction
yet it is

        afflicting everything.

Rime of the Ancient Mariners

What kind of people spend all day
picking up on the most subtle signs of displeasure

from everyone else
        with all the sorrow of Berryman

that cherished alcoholic, drunk-dialing his student in the
    middle of the night
and threatening to kill her—

                            his fragile and unending barrel
of shame that, when opened,
proved to be unoccupied.

Save him for the one hawk, or

the clean gray wing he couldn't handle, the bane
of his existence was his tiny

mouth   that was stuck to him—

Now, tell me, what kind of person
            says: *tomorrow, tomorrow, tomorrow*

every day before she falls asleep,
like a prayer in reverse,
                            like the ancient mariner
whose immediate guilt

is useless,
       selfish even,
ignoring everything else

and managing, always, to make everything
worse. Tell me, who is that looking out

from that crow's nest,
from that widow's walk?

What kind of person
       can be found standing in one spot in the snow
until all the skin is gone

       and there's only a dismal luster, breaking apart?

O Wedding Guest!

I pass, like night, from land to land;
I have strange power of speech

—Samuel Taylor Coleridge, "The Rime of
the Ancient Mariner"

Rippling outward—
I cannonball into the chasm—
soaking the onlookers with wet shadow—
wormhole to nowhere—

torn hem of my wedding dress
thrown into the mouths
thrown into the mouths
of babes and sucklings—

And what manner of woman am I?
Worn of the institution of marriage.
A ghastly tale I tell myself.
My hands are hands in the middle

of some dark prayer.
Belief ties me to the mast.
The maelstrom sucks me down.
I'm lost in the *Carta marina*—

glorious illuminated map
that even I can look upon
and see the lurid pull
of imperialism—

I am lost in the legislature.
Western literature, here be
monsters—my own mutant guests—
and all love must perish—

do not forgive me.

Dear Sir or Madam

I saw your dog on the side of the road.
His features gone
but I recognized the coloring.
There was no shoulder to pull over onto.
I carry no shovel.
My sense of direction is okay,
but my fear of stopping on a highway—
I can't tell you
how sorry I am. We are all only this.
We are roused by thunder,
tortured into pleasure by lightning,
fertilized by the wind and rain,
raised up by the sun,
dismembered by the moon.

Set Designer

Once, Mark Leidner talked me into doing set design,
unpaid, in the Poconos
where I would be forever traumatized
by the overpopulation of deer,
growths on their bodies and bald patches,
limping and scarred from being hit by cars,
and the one the crew called "jawbone"
that kept coming around
because its jawbone was hanging off, unusable, from its head
while the body wasted away
and I brought out mashed potatoes
that it lapped up with a long tongue.

We had to fire the creepy sound guy
who was clearly on drugs
and I found a big plastic gallon of Dewer's
in the Airbnb cupboard
and a guitar
and got drunk alone on the deck of the cabin
amazed no one would join me.
I woke in the middle of the night
for my usual routine of self-hatred
until I realized how excruciating it all was
and instead wrote down on the set schedule
"remember how good it feels to be good to yourself"

carrying it around with me ever since.
Hoping I will.

Dark Mad Stallion

Here we have come.

    I have ended on the back of a dark mad stallion

who drags me all over my hometown.

    Everything corrodes in our wake.

He frees himself.

And with an ancient tattered rope
hanging from the bit

    he leaves me standing alone.

They caught him by the high school

      they keep him in a huge wire cage

I go to see him sometimes

                    rage
                    spreads his shimmering black coat

            I bring
things   little offerings

                            I put carrots

through the holes
            and sometimes my finger gets in
            and he bites down hard.

TRIAD

Tragic Nature

Your three-year-old has found you
sitting in the kitchen.
(You can hardly speak when you are like this.)

She pauses. Asks why you are sad,
climbs onto the counter
and begins siphoning something into

the corner of your mouth
with a plastic play syringe.
Lemonade, it turns out.

The sugar enters you like Naloxone.
She is the one alive, holding up.
Now the huge cowbird, your illness,

a ravenous changeling in the sparrow nest
stirs uneasily. You, the sow who eats her piglets
because she is tired

of the whole succession of things.
Grubbing in their invincible
soft skin, glass eyes, fresh breath.

It is hard for mothers to be like this.
It is hard for mothers to be sick
like this.

Across the field, frogs have climbed out
from the pond and onto Route 7
in an evening rainstorm.

The pavement steams.
The frog silhouettes fling left and right
like a child's wall decal

into the evening traffic,
long stream of bright twin spotlights—
their lives are brief.

The road the next day
is littered with them.
The smashed twisted bodies of young frogs.

Wolves

Well, where are you?

Virginia Woolf would begin her letters
to Vita Sackville-West. Or

Here is another selfish invalids bulletin.

Which is how I feel
staring at a black-and-white photograph
of an arctic wolf.

Though it is not the greatest of compositions
(too much is faded, unclear)
it arrests every part of me.

The bare, depressing winter trees
against the bloomed gray-white sky
suit me.

The wolf's footpads in the snow
disappear into
haggard whiteness.

From a removed, righteous vantage point
as viewer
I realize we are meant to be the photographer.

And I assume the wolf is female because
she looks right at me
from her confine of light and chemicals on paper,

some part of her soul
burned onto the paper like a nuclear shadow—
and that is how women look

when seen suddenly
from the wilds of their private, difficult life.

You Could Spend Every Night with the Television

The uneasiness of being alive wears you down.
So, you might sit with the television.
Your obligatory interview.
Fatal, in its mirrored posture.
One musical interlude after another.
All the universes of *Star Trek*
you haven't mastered. The unreal
digitally rendered areas of planet Earth
you will never enter. You sit down with it
like the detective who knows
way less than she's letting on
sits across from the cantankerous yet somehow
absurdly fearless criminal.
You'll be there all night, bluffing each other.
You could spend a lifetime
eating dried fruit
and nuts and wine
like an apostle resentful of the flock
in its huge vision
and not even fight the urge
to be given a better story
with all its core-crew immortality
and moral surrender. You'll accept it.

Sit down as an equal in its light.
Sit like a painting that faces a window.
Try to cancel each other out.

Beatrices

How can we follow a vision,
manifest in cloth and be loved?
The Beatrices want to know.

Anger that refuses its own knowledge.
Oh, his terrible odes went beneath my nails.
I, into the tight circles of Hell with him,

flattered, I let him
cannibalize my face, my hands.
Let him worship me for his own vanity.

(For no muse gets to be real to herself.)
The personality raped for years,
shredded like a milkweed husk.

How can you blame me?
I wanted to be loved right.
I wanted to pilgrim that

unknown territory. I wanted
to witness the creator love his conception.
But it soured me. I made garlands of that pain.

Adorned the mirror with it.
Now, I stand transfixed before it.
Beatrice implodes in me

who too is made of that sentient
livid dust.

Quantum Theorists in 1926

It had been unnecessary to *see*
a picture of a nuclear atom back then;
each scientist held a vivid
mental picture
and from imagination of the atom
framed complex experiments.
But Schrödinger's equation
that beautifully described
how wave function works
gave no hint on how
it could be imagined.

I am not the time-evolution operator.
And cannot frame my days.
Cannot quite picture
the problem; awkward and
untranslatable, it comes
as a dizziness, suffocating
and shapeless, another kind
of wave.

It seems lately that everything is nearing its end.
Everyone keeps saying so.
How we throw off the balance,
how we are

the tragic mistake of Nature.
And I'm still stuck listing
all the things I will miss when it goes.
The inconstant equation of us.
The way we theorize about what lasts.
How we don't have to get it
to understand one another.
How when Schrödinger finally
painted the wave picture in full detail,
if anything, it made it all
less clear.

Marriage

Do all husbands sit in their offices
with *Evangelion*, sorting Magic cards,
reading *Deadspin*, scoffing?
Something died in the walls upstairs, I tell him.
The air conditioner sits on the floor.
Like a morgue the bedroom hides bodies.
Remains unpainted. The mirror sits on the floor.
Lush goldenrod dampening to brown.
The night is clearest when no one is out.
But at 2 AM I rise when he finally comes to bed.
I pull the garbage cans down the long grassy driveway.
I see it all up there. It yawns before me,
a demon of baryonic matter, average atoms,
energy, dark fuzz, and it calms me—

O perilous, altruistic mute god of love.

(Not) the Last Television Poem

Whose is that noble, dauntless brow?
Television, you great time waster.
A miracle! A thousand flapping frames
of miracles, piling up on one another.

I'm vanishing altogether inside
a myth of perpetual nemeses.
Two implacable forces
clinging to distinctiveness

and we the meek,
subscribing, in a spasm of terror!

The Wealth

The truth is
money is in war, not poetry.
Money is in real estate and clean water.
Money is in other people's money.
Not pitted antique linens
with slight stains at the hand stitch
Mom swears are "worth a lot."
Money is in country, in USA! In Fiction,
in the numbered ether.
Not square nails rusted brittle to the touch
kept in tin cans around the house
for the strange subversive opulence
of one day "selling."

Money is not in our wistful, near-mint antiques.
More critically, it is not in abstinence. In blank
space between ink. Absorbed by a single cell
when all the mind wants is to indulge—
money is not in *not* indulging. Not in
the flushed ranks of your crippled piety.

I will miss money. Miss lush foliage.
The abundance of summer.
I will miss apples and asters and frogs,
the smell of weed, the acridness of body,

when we drive ourselves out of luck with cars.
Money is an abstract scream, not
the silence that hangs from the head
in a broken nimbus,
lighting near the edge of what you know.

I know nothing of money. Of wealth.
And from the torqued maw comes
bitter truths, The wading bird that thinks
it can eat the ocean. Our becoming
that has gone septic. Money is in the oasis,
in mirage and delirious hunt.

Mary Magdalene

Where was it—

      Just a moment ago

            I swear it was here.

Now I am alone in the office.
In Peter's gospels

with the lions, an unworthy female.

But all desire springs from the pit.

Hungry pleaser,
        eaten alive.   Upright in death—

Is it discipline? The disciples?

          Hung by the foot, flayed by beauty?

And where are you, beloved?

Beloved?

Skin and hair
stretched across the land

riddled with trained lice—
you are too deep inside me.

Wallpapered in my subconscious.

Prayer is a thin   ambassador,

an anorexic in the fourth dimension.

Like waves against the stalwarts—
or the rapport between fish and coral reefs—

we live like this,
darting in and out
of the lion's hot mouth

to the thunderous applause
of the multitude.

Where was it? It was just here . . .   I had it
in my forehead—her
beauty—it

      spun around   in me, a total annihilation of
spirit—it

baptized me
then dropped me back

into the magnificent, terrifying illusion

of ordinary   thought.

The Request of the Doe

The old doe wanted to be witnessed in pain for eternity.
Cut and bandaged and then cut up again.
Fine, they said. We'll see how you fare.
They took her into the sterile room and covered her in dirt.
They smothered her in praise.
They pulled out her teeth and replaced them
with all gold caps over steel rod implants.
They propped her up on an ancestor's grave
and told her to be still as a stone.

The stone wanted to be witnessed for eternity.
Carved as it was. Like a great mysterious henge.
But it was clear who placed her there.
And that wasn't enough. No one wants to see
that which they already see every day in the mirror.
Tricked out and suffering. Cut up for no one.
Those teeth shone in the night for no one.
When she bore them at the moon.

TETRAD

Other Wound

The wound is usually someone else's.
My love was never enough.
I couldn't touch the whole of it.
I wasn't a match for that depth.

Every daughter
has a cage around her head
and a mother on the cross.

I always hope to take it off, and rarely do.
Instead, I climb up, like a child into the bed.
I nail myself beside you.

Pain as White Paint

They say it is necessary for women to forget.
Every second she is forgetting a little more,
though it is always in the back of her mind.
Even after the epidural kicked in, you started to forget
and let it wear off, then remembered again, then forgot again.
Horrible pain is like that.

But you remember the reaction to the pain
that was so shrill
it couldn't be fathomed in terms of normal comprehension.

It translated into the conceptual.
It became a symposium.
Something historic. A context and citizenry of agony,
it peopled and weaved its own life,
and in sorcery unpacked
unfathomable waves of itself into the high and low offices

while you watched
detached, yet linked, from the front row.
A courtside celebrity feeling everything in the basketball.
Each wave seemingly identical yet utterly unique
they smashed you head to toe, for literal hours,
what seemed couldn't get worse, always did
in some ingenious way,

always reverting back to a basic idea of *pain*; and
in reaching a pitch, the contractions
became
          white paint,
particularly, you thought, on the side of the barn,
they became a white wall with no top, no bottom or edge
as if trying to understand what you were seeing
looking from some other reality
through a fixed lens.

The Infant's Eyes

Now that I too am
the terrible witness
to the ovum
and I have been
wrestled to the ground
with her fresh bread
and dirt
breath and have been
the laughing maniac
of motherhood
now
I will always
rise and go
to see what is wrong
like a cardinal to the pope
whenever something sounds
from upstairs
I'll rush up
or out
or in
to see what is what
whether anyone is hurt
or in need
then I will putter back
to continue the leftover

saggy and unreal job
of aging
toward benediction.

Now
when I bite into
the tied-off end
of a sausage
it reminds me
of her umbilical cord.
As the eyes
of the mice
in my kitchen
remind me of her eyes
in the unclearness
of the birthing room—
when the mice watch me
storm about, slamming
dishes, it reminds me
how her infant eyes
began
to follow me
when I paced
the little
horrible apartment

we were living in
when she was born
an apartment
that reeked in the hallway
of cigarettes
and the neighbor was always
screaming at her boyfriend
that he was
"making her fat"
because he didn't
love her enough
and he would hang
out his window
smoking a bowl
saying "Geezus
fuckinChrist"
and shaking
his head

those were the days
when my baby began
following me with her eyes
when I—neurotic
about her breathing—noticed her
noticing me—

and realized I'd never been
looked at like that before.
As if the sky
had ripped off
a strip of its blue
and a massive face
looked through at me—
I froze under her
dispassionate
infant stare

her twin black crystal balls
focusing fully on me
surveying like
an ancient god
the status
of evolution's
latest results,
making what
could only be
her
Edenic judgments.

Mockingbird

After weeks of silence
its first words were
Talk! Damn you, talk!

Its imitation of my mother's cry
so precise I can't tell it from the real thing.

I love her. It is just that
I am so afraid of the obvious fact

that there is always more to know
of suffering.

Does the mockingbird have its own call?
Lost in the repertoire, she will always repeat
the songs of the damned.

You can tell where a mockingbird has been
by the songs she sings.

Niente amo

Falstaff in all forms but wit,
I'm my dead lapdog, Niente,
licking a cat food can on the floor
of my mother's house.
That dog killed me every time
she got stuck at the top of the stairs
and whimpered to be carried down. Or when
we pulled and pulled at her nipple
thinking it was a tick—now, she pulls at mine
from beyond the grave.
Her little body of tumors, her daily eyedrops
I always forgot; searching around
for something to eat, waiting to be let out
then just squatting in my closet to piss
again until the floor got soft and dark.
Sometimes, nowadays, her purebred hair,
matted and greasy, blows around the room
when I think I am alone,
appears like a freak snowstorm.
We were brittle survivors in the cave.
We were prose, suitable for comic
low-status characters, or disguise, *sirra*,
unbrushed, I used to
cling to her at night
like the ice in her fur would

in dense white dangling balls—
when I think I am alone
when I think I am okay
sometimes, nowadays, she shivers
and barks from the veil,
waiting to be fed my heart again.

The Ostensible Psychic Wound

The trick is to sew it up with a single hair
from your mother's head
with a needle whittled out of an eyelash
from your first-grade teacher
who said once she "missed the old Bianca."
Sew it up tight and then move on.
Rather than spend a lifetime attempting
to equal its sore.
Seal it up with hardening oatmeal.
Drink a bucket of cold water from the brook.
Fast for forty days, on the movement
of the crows around the merlin.
And wherever you step
be sure no blade of grass will care.
No insect would follow. No lover will stalk. It is
okay. What you wanted was wrong,
but also, totally understandable. Join us
at the midnight service
in all shiny black and empty rubber Jesus masks
and we will do your favorite thing:
light a little candle on the person beside you
until the whole fucking world is holding fire
from a single source,
and you will not be the only one anymore,

but rather, one of the many
many ones—where there is
nothing between cured and wounded.

Twins

Mom says our father had to sit on her
to keep her from the abortion clinic.
He left anyway, when it was too late
to give us back. My brother came first.
Now I want to lead him to where Hafiz
signed his poems in the poem. That is
what it is like to be born—to have the poet's
name written into you. Even if you didn't want it.

My brother and I looked hard for the house
of sweets, lost in the woods, confusing starvation
for gluttony, and we swore again
we wouldn't, but always did, stuffing ourselves
and suffering—and now I deem
our longing to be a longing to be listened to
by Nature: the unmoved mother
beautiful at her boudoir, lathered in her face mask
of decayed butterflies and lava,
her oubliette eyes and casual irises
looking over the menu, ordering nothing.

Ecstatic, my brother and I age simultaneously.
We twin-out poems in real time. We are
parallel lines with two fixed points behind us.
Somehow, we keep on going. Kind of rare.
Usually drunk. An obscure collector's set.

Quantum Mechanics Reveals the Unique Behaviors of Subatomic Particles That Make Up All Matter

I've disappeared into the huge false teeth of my grandma's mouth
hoping she'll posthumously forgive me for our fight
when she shouted so hard, they fell out.
"You don't like me anymore
because you found out I have dentures,"
she said later. I was the crocodile stunned shut.
My love could never be
fully trusted.

Unique behaviors between mothers and daughters
are like the behaviors between subatomic particles
that make up all matter.
Yanked into the car. Beet-red. Broke.

I blow upon the tiny glass beads. I scatter them on the floor.
The image appears, shudders, disappears.
I feast as if on fresh snow. I feast on the song of it all.

During the Nap

A ball of light at the perineum
makes its way to the skull
like an air bubble in the vein.
Your daughter is sleeping.
Her lashes down
like the fringe of piano shawls.
Her fingers point at an angle
like a Giotto. She is sleeping
and for a moment
you are free.
But all you can do is wait
and watch.

It is all your fault.
That she is stunning
and innocent.
You are the battery
inside the frightening bear
that speaks and sings
like an evangelical when shook.
You're the freak at the gate
who will do anything
for the tiny mad queen.
The sniper in the tower
with no name.

A Queen's Ransom

I used to think myself such the righteous
defender of dandelions. But every weed takes its turn.
I rubbed them on everyone's chin
for the stolen child
who whipped the rushing river with her golden hair
drowned leaves and unquieted mothers' dreams
I'd left her
for my own essential source of panic
in the error of my evolution
I'd lost something, maybe never
had it—sure that my body had something to do with it
our espousing self
the androgynous animus
kept warm with bread and olive oil, burned
but raw at the core
I do not know what else to do
honored and revered, cult-like with our own despair
around and around the same impasse.

What are your personal disciples like?
Children wandering in someone else's field.
I am almost totally deaf. All I can hear
is the harshest of birds—crows, blue jays—
the pounding washing machines, buzzes of the phones—
everything nonessential comes through.

Nettle and pigweed.   I see it
like a boat on the empty lake
rowing its empty passengers toward me.

I'm tired of wine, tired of trying.
It's like
          there are the canonical gospels.
And then there's the oral tradition of screaming.

Yellow Balloon

Odette wanted her yellow balloon back
although it was pitch-black

and her eyes were closed
and there is nothing that would return

such a gift. And the next morning even I
had to harden my heart

at the residential pest-control services
outside on my sister's front porch

as if it were something
to be achieved. But it is

a refusal of God
that torments me. Wasps

fighting in formation
and dying. How all we do

is move from meal to meal.
Drink to drink. It is not even syphilis. It is

the human state. A kind of
psychosis of sadness

of being in a world
we cannot bow to.

Cutting Odette's Fingernails

Who is the barber
with the straight razor
at the neck of the Mad King
or the physician of the Don
who must hold him fast between the legs.
Who are the parents without
sensation, except their own
irreparable, endless burning,
who cannot fathom any other way—
what jobs we get ourselves into.
We are never ready.
I feel like at this moment
I could be anyone in the world
because I could be, with a
a hundred objects
of torture—*whatever*
the mind can come up with
has been done, I read
somewhere and cannot
forget—broken and healed, submerged
in saltwater and ice, waiting
to be brought back
like the peat-bog murder victims
into a century of data.
I didn't come to perdition

I changed perdition—
stood stock-still
and changed
abyss—planted something
in the dust bowl
made abandoned
by the blinding sun
and let loose cattle
knowing I used to get
obliterated and wander
the streets of New York
looking for takeout
a pair of scissors, waiting
to open me like a lily
I used to bang my head
against the wall
the audience
the neighbors
used to dream it
and do it
wineglasses in the sink
against one another
in my bare hands
the world was clay
worked into something

too heavy to carry—
I had to *let* blood, was
the physician of my own
imbalanced humors
I experimented
all that misuse
and it seems so insane now,
finally, it feels unclear
in my mouth
with this vowel
that has come off me
like a soap bubble
this target of glory
a tiny bright oligarch
an opium substance
of my chromosomes
who first almost comprehended
the full moon while I held her
in a field on a mountain,
pointed at it and said *ball*—
now her infant hand
is palm-down on my knee
like a starfish, and
her translucent fingernails
fall to ground

like the husks of stars
wished upon, granted,
forgiven for whatever
defeat seemed so important
for so long—that desire
to be laid out on the marble
and sewn back up—
no, it all went differently—
I see it now; how
we tend to hold pain
so close, as if
it is all
we're made of.

In Absence—This Unknowing

When you leave, faceless
old lover, element
that I have tried for so long
to explain—I will be
suspended between
two large stones
for a moment
thinking you were good
before I am revived.
I will be laundry
that has gotten loose
from the line. Pantyhose
flying into traffic.
So long, handsome.
When you go, I will be
the moth, the butterfly,
turned to broth in the cocoon.
Reassembled, I will climb out
and you will be subsumed
into a majesty of vapor
gone as an orchid.
I plan it, little switchblade.
I will it, strand of sweet spittle,
endearing idiot I made
out of mud and loss—

you, whose shelf life is zero,
you, who keep me from totality
and the small sum of what
is otherwise infinite.

A Suckling Pig's Prayer

I have put aside all the blank meaningless words
and decided to go, totally naked
into the always luscious Elysian dump
of the hereafter. Say nothing at all.

May the wind take all this hair. Dissolve
these shallow scars, tear
whatever cloth is left hanging
between my legs and water, absorb me
into your passive liquid rush,

forget the marrow and calcium, the dust,
the single chaotic fluid—old pure
and muddy wind, leave me a shocked afterimage—
windblast even that still-quivering outline,
that empty silhouette the paper doll left behind—

to remember me
may my portrait be of an elderly nun
with a pitted face, rooting blindly
for the stone's breast of blood-black buttermilk—

Do not box me up like the ancient queens of Thebes
in gilded wood, alabaster, and obsidian.
Leave no trace of what sibling rivalry
occurred between us, the one who stood half
in shadow. Who made these words.

Acknowledgments

The occurrence of a book is a conversation. The essential editing journey undertaken during 2020–2021 was a personally transformative one that is mirrored in these poems. I would like to thank the people who were part of this conversation. I would like to thank my Tin House editors, Elizabeth and Alyssa, who were rigorous and indispensable; the RSH Tuesday night workshop; Candace Jensen, in an alchemical, illuminated embrace; James Barnes, for our dialogue about the "inside-out-part-experience-magical-conjuring-of-the-individual-psyche"; Leanne Ruell, whose beauty, poetry and relentless inquiry into experience keeps me authentic and our friendship epic—may we continue philosophizing together, ad infinitum; Elizabeth Powell and Alison Prine, for wonderful early feedback on the book. Thank you to Jeffery A., PA-C, for steering me in a direction that changed everything. Thank you Andrew M. for helping me think the unthinkable. And again, my family, Ben Pease, Walter Stone, and Odette Stone-Pease, in whose orbit this gratitude and love is most vivid and infinite.

Poem Dedications & References

"Does Life Exist Independent of Its Form?" is dedicated to my sister, Hillery.

"Apocrypha" was written in a style after Mark Leidner's "Biographies of Einstein," from his book *Beauty Was the Case That They Gave Me* (Factory Hollow Press, 2011).

"After Getting Advice to Look out the Window & Say 'Thank You'" is dedicated to Ben Fama.

"Psychodynamic Motivational Speech" is dedicated to Andrew M.

Gratitude to the magazines where these poems, in some form or another, were first published or are forthcoming:

Poetry: "Marcus Aurelius," "Cutting Odette's Fingernails"

The Baffler: "Routine" (published as "Morning Routine"), "The Wealth"

The New Yorker: "Nature," "The Way Things Were Until Now" (published as "The Way Things Were Up Until Now"), "Artichokes"

Powder Keg: "God Searches for God," "Drunk during Creation"

jubilat: "I'll Tell You"

Pigeon Pages: "After Getting Advice to Look out the Window & Say 'Thank You'"

The Nation: "Request of the Doe"

Isele Magazine: "During the Nap," "A Queen's Ransom"

Washington Square Review: "Yellow Balloon"

MORE BOOKS BY
BIANCA STONE

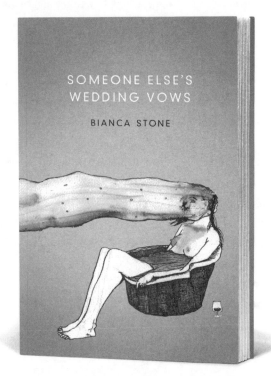

"Bianca Stone's poetry has the glow of twenty-first-century enlightenment and lyric possession. Hilarious and powerful."

—MAJOR JACKSON